GW01185245

Basic
FRENCH
Grammar

John Corbett
Formerly Director of Education, Luton

Anne Johnson
Formerly Head of Modern Languages Department
Howell's School, Denbigh

John Murray Albemarle Street London

© John Corbett and Anne Johnson 1975

First published 1975
Reprinted (revised) 1976, 1979, 1981

Printed in Hong Kong by Wing King Tong Co., Ltd.

0 7195 2913 1

Contents

ADJECTIVES 2

ADVERBS

NEGATIVES

PREPOSITIONS

VERBS

Nouns

1 Definite and indefinite articles

French nouns are either masculine or feminine in gender. The gender of a noun is usually, but not always, connected with its historical derivation.

The **definite** and **indefinite** articles are

	Definite (the)		Indefinite (a, an)	
	Singular	*Plural*	*Singular*	*Plural*
masculine	**le, l'**	**les**	**un**	
feminine	**la, l'**	**les**	**une**	**de(s)**

2

The **l'** form of the definite article is used when the noun begins with a vowel: **l'air, l'école** (exception – **onze** and its derivatives: **le onze mai** – the 11th of May) or with what is technically called a non-aspirate 'h', e.g. **l'honneur.** There is in fact no aspirate 'h' in French as there is in English and the nouns beginning with 'h' which require **le** or **la** are best learnt as they occur; among the common ones are

la haine	hatred	**le héros**	hero (but **l'héroïne**)
le hareng	herring	**le hêtre**	beech
le hibou	owl	**le hollandais**	Dutch
la honte	shame	**la houille**	coal
la hutte	hut	**le haricot**	bean
le huit	the eight	**le homard**	lobster
		la hauteur	height

the adjective **haut** as in **le haut Canada** Upper Canada

Note: (a) **un/une** are not used with nouns describing vocations or professions after **il (elle) est (était** etc.**).**

Il est médecin	but	**C'est un médecin**
Elle est institutrice	but	**C'est une institutrice**

(b) No article is required with **avec** and **sans** if the noun is not qualified.

Thus **Il agit avec courage** but **Il agit avec un courage farouche**
Elle s'est mariée sans dot

(c) In some proverbs the article is omitted

Pierre qui roule n'amasse pas mousse	A rolling stone gathers no moss

(d) | | |
|---|---|
| **Je l'ai pour ami** | I have him as *a* friend |
| **Elle le prendra pour guide** | She will take him as *a* guide |
| **Elle m'a traité en ennemi** | She treated me as *an* enemy |

(e) When nouns are in apposition the definite article is not used with the second noun

Londres, capitale de l'Angleterre	London, the capital of England
Louis XIV, roi de France	Louis XIV, the King of France

3 The **partitive article** expresses the idea of 'some', 'any'. It is not always represented by a word in English

Il mange de la viande	He is eating meat

The partitive article is

	Singular	*Plural*
masculine	**du, de l', de**	**des, de**
feminine	**de la, de l', de**	**des, de**

Elle achète du jambon	She's buying some ham
Elle n'achète pas de jambon	She is not buying any ham
Nous avons du succès	We have some success
Nous n'avons jamais de succès	We never have any success
Je vois des pigeons sur le toit	I see some pigeons on the roof
Je ne vois plus de pigeons sur le toit	I can't see any more pigeons on the roof

Thus the partitive idea after a negative is represented by **de** only.

4 If an adjective precedes a plural noun the partitive must be rendered by **de** only

J'ai de bons amis dans ce village	I have some good friends in this village

4

But **des** is used when the adjective and noun, often found together, seem to form a new noun

On y voit des jeunes filles	You can see girls there
Je vais acheter des petits pains	I'm going to buy some rolls

When the noun is in the singular and the adjective precedes, use **du, de l', de la**

Il y a du bon vin ici	There's good wine here

5 Gender

Nouns which relate to male creatures are almost always masculine; those relating to female creatures, feminine

le taureau	the bull	**la vache**	the cow
le coiffeur	hairdresser (man)	**la coiffeuse**	hairdresser (woman)
le Juif	Jew	**la Juive**	Jewess
le veuf	widower	**la veuve**	widow

but note: 1.

la sentinelle	sentry
la recrue	recruit
une femme député	a woman M.P.
une femme médecin	a woman doctor
une femme professeur	a woman teacher

2. **gens** is masculine plural but adjectives *before* it are feminine

ces gens sont sots   but   de sottes gens

6 Nouns with the following endings are masculine

- age	**le courage**
- ier	**le sucrier**
- oir	**l'abreuvoir**
- at	**le candidat**
- isme	**le fascisme**

except: **la rage, cage, nage, plage, image, page** (in a book)

7 Parts of speech not originally nouns but used as nouns, are masculine

le rire   laugh

le sourire	smile
le oui	the yes, affirmative
le rouge et le noir	the red and the black

8 Nouns with the following endings are feminine

- ade	**la promenade**	
- ance	**la tolérance**	
- ion	**l'apparition**	except: **le bastion**
- oire	**une écritoire**	except: **le Directoire**
- trice	**la directrice**	
- ière	**la cafetière**	

Diminutives ending in
- ette	**la maisonnette**

9 Countries, continents and provinces ending in - **e** are feminine

la belle Espagne	except: **le Mexique**
la Provence	

10 Nouns of either gender

l'après-midi
l'enfant ⎫
l'élève ⎭ according to sex

11 The following nouns are masculine and feminine — varying according
to meaning

le moule	mould	**la moule**	mussel
le poêle	stove	**la poêle**	dish
le vase	vase	**la vase**	mud
le mousse	cabin boy	**la mousse**	moss
le poste	post (job)	**la poste**	post (mail)
le page	page (servant)	**la page**	page (in a book)

12 **Plurals of nouns** — in general plurals are made by adding 's' but

(a) nouns ending in -**s**, -**x**, -**z** make no change in the plural
le nez	**les nez**

(b) nouns ending in **-al** make their plural in **-aux**

journal   **journaux**

except: **aval, bal, carnaval, chacal, choral, festival, narval, récital, régal** which make plurals by adding **-s**

(c) nouns ending in **-ail** make their plural in **-aux**

émail	**émaux**
travail	**travaux**

(d) nouns ending in **-eu**, **-eau** make plurals by adding **-x**

bateau	**bateaux**
neveu	**neveux**

Note: **pneu** makes plural **pneus** — because it is an abbreviated form of **pneu(matique)s**

(e) the following nouns in **-ou** make their plural in **-oux**

bijou	**chou**	**hibou**	**pou**
caillou	**genou**	**joujou**	

(f) **aïeul** has two plurals:

aïeuls	grandfathers
aïeux	more remote ancestors

(g)

un oeil	**des yeux**	but	**des oeils de bœuf**	
le bœuf	**les bœufs**		the 'f' is pronounced in the singular but not in the plural

(h) The following nouns occur in the plural only

arrhes	pledge, deposit	**obsèques**	obsequies
fiançailles	betrothal	**ténèbres**	darkness
funérailles	funeral ceremony	**vacances**	holidays

13   Plurals of **compound nouns**

Whether one puts neither element, one or the other, or both into the plural depends on the logic of the situation.

Thus

un timbre-poste	**des timbres-poste**	presumably because they are **timbres pour la poste**
un coffre-fort	**des coffres-forts**	because the adjective applies to the noun in the plural and therefore agrees with it

un haut-parleur	des haut-parleurs	because here haut is used adverbially
un tête-à-tête	des tête-à-tête	because the whole noun is really an adverbial phrase
un laissez-passer	des laissez-passer	because the whole noun is really a verbal expression

except

un pourboire	des pourboires	the sense of there being two parts has been lost by long usage
un passeport	des passeports	

Remember:

un monsieur	des messieurs
madame	mesdames
mademoiselle	mesdemoiselles
un bonhomme	des bonshommes
un gentilhomme	des gentilshommes

14 In combined nouns linked by a preposition à stresses purpose

une tasse à thé	a tea cup (a cup for the purpose of drinking tea)
un moulin à café	a coffee mill
une boîte à bijoux	a jewel box

à also indicates an agent of propulsion

une machine à vapeur	a steam engine
un moulin à vent	a windmill

When the material is used in construction the preposition is usually en

une montre en argent	a silver watch
une chaise en bois	a wooden chair
une maison en briques	a brick house

but de is used with some nouns

un pont de pierre	a stone bridge
une route de béton	a concrete road

8

Possessive Adjectives

Person			One owner					More than one owner	
			Singular	*Plural*				*Singular*	*Plural*
1	my	*m.*	mon		our	*m.*		notre	nos
		f.	ma	mes		*f.*			
2	your	*m.*	ton		your	*m.*		votre	vos
	(thy)	*f.*	ta*	tes		*f.*			
3	his	*m.*	son		their	*m.*		leur	leurs
	her	*f.*	sa*	ses		*f.*			
	its								

mon père ⎫
ma mère ⎭   mes parents   notre père   nos parents

* the masculine form is used to avoid a clash of vowels, when the noun or preceding adjective begins with a vowel or a mute 'h'

son autre soeur, ton orange, son honnêteté

Note: use of **mon** with military ranks

         Oui, mon capitaine!   Yes, sir!

and with religious 'family' names

         Oui, mon père   (to a priest)

         Non, ma soeur   (to a nun)

Demonstrative Adjectives

16

Demonstrative adjectives, like other adjectives, agree with their noun in number and gender. There are two forms: the simple and the (more emphatic) compound one.

		Singular	*Plural*	
Simple	*m.*	ce, cet*	ces	this, that,
	f.	cette		these, those

		Singular	*Plural*	
Compound	*m.*	ce (noun) -ci	ces (noun) -ci	this, these
		cet* (noun) -ci		
		ce (noun) -la	ces (noun) -là	that, those
		cet* (noun) -la		
	f.	cette (noun) -ci	ces (noun) -ci	this, these
		cette (noun) -la	ces (noun) -là	that, those
		* before a vowel or mute 'h'		

The suffix -ci is a corruption of ici and indicates that the noun is near, i.e. it makes an emphatic form of 'this', 'these'. The suffix -là is the adverb là and obviously indicates that the noun is further away, i.e. it makes an emphatic form of 'that', 'those'.

Je ne pouvais pas distinguer ces hommes-là à deux cents mètres	I couldn't distinguish those men two hundred yards away
Cet animal-ci est moins dangereux que ce serpent-là	This animal is less dangerous than that snake

Numbers

17 Cardinal

0 zéro

1 un	11 onze	21 vingt et un	31 trente et un
2 deux	12 douze	22 vingt-deux	32 trente-deux
3 trois	13 treize	23 vingt-trois	etc.
4 quatre	14 quatorze	etc.	
5 cinq	15 quinze		
6 six	16 seize		
7 sept	17 dix-sept		
8 huit	18 dix-huit		
9 neuf	19 dix-neuf		
10 dix	20 vingt	30 trente	40 quarante

41 quarante et un	50 cinquante	60 soixante
42 quarante-deux	51 cinquante et un	61 soixante et un
	52 cinquante-deux	62 soixante-deux

70 soixante-dix	80 quatre-vingts	90 quatre-vingt-dix
71 soixante et onze	81 quatre-vingt-un	91 quatre-vingt-onze
72 soixante-douze	82 quatre-vingt-deux	92 quatre-vingt-douze
73 soixante-treize		

100 cent	101 cent un	1,000 mille
200 deux cents	201 deux cent un	1,001 mille un
300 trois cents	302 trois cent deux	

Note: (a) the 's' on the French is used only for the following round numbers: 80, 200, 300 etc.

(b) in dates of the modern era mil instead of mille
   mil soixante-six   1066

but dates beyond the XI century are usually given in hundreds
   dix-neuf cent soixante-douze   1972

18 Ordinal - formed usually by adding -ième to the cardinal

le premier, la première	first	**le, la neuvième**	ninth
le, la deuxième	second	**le, la dixième**	tenth
le, la troisième	third	**le, la vingtième**	twentieth
le, la quatrième	fourth	**le, la vingt et unième**	twenty-first
le, la cinquième	fifth	etc.	

Note:

Dates	Kings		Chapters
(a) **le premier mai**	**Charles Premier**	Charles I	**Chapitre premier**
le deux mai	**Charles Deux**	Charles II	**Chapitre deux**
le onze mai	**Louis Quatorze**	Louis XIV	**Chapitre trois**
le trente et un mai			

(b) **le second, la seconde** - is generally used instead of **le, la deuxième** when there is no reference to third, fourth, fifth etc.

une nouvelle de seconde main	a second-hand piece of news
Elle était d'une beauté sans seconde	She was of an unrivalled beauty

19 Other numbers

1. **-aine,** meaning approximate numbers of quantities

une dizaine	about 10	**une douzaine**	a dozen
une quinzaine	about 15 (also = a fortnight)		
but: **un millier**	a group of about 1000		

2. fractions:

un demi	⎱	**un tiers**	$\frac{1}{3}$
une demie	⎰ ½	**un quart**	¼
une moitié		**trois quarts**	¾

Note: **demi** preceding does not agree; following, it does

une demi-bouteille	half a bottle
une bouteille et demie	a bottle and a half
une demi-heure	half an hour
Il est deux heures et demie	It is half past two

demi as a noun is in arithmetic only; otherwise use **moitié**

'half' used adverbially + adjective is **à moitié**

Elle était à moitié nue	She was half-naked

Pronouns

20   **Personal pronouns** are of two kinds

1. **Ordinary** - used as the non-emphatic subject or the object of verbs

		1 *m. & f.*	2 *m. & f.*	3 *m.*	*f.*	
Subject	*sg.*	je	tu	il	elle	
	pl.	nous	vous	ils	elles	
Object	*sg.*	me, m'	te, t'	le, l'	la, l'	
(direct)	*pl.*	nous	vous	les	les	
Object	*sg.*	me, m'	te, t'	lui	lui	usually standing
(indirect)	*pl.*	nous	vous	leur	leur	for à + noun

Ils ont donné le prix à Charles	They gave the prize to Charles *or* They gave Charles the prize
Ils le lui ont donné	They gave it *to him*
Voici la fleur! Elle la leur avait donnée	Here is the flower! She had given it to them

Note: 1. In compound tenses the past participle agrees with any *preceding direct* object. This is often a personal pronoun as in the last example (therefore **donnée**) but not always so

La rose que j'ai cueillie	The rose I gathered

2. **le** may stand for an adjective

Ton père était fier	Your father was proud
Essaie de l'être aussi	Try to be (so) too

Note: for position of pronouns with a verb see paragraph 163

21   **Form of address: tu** is the singular form between close relatives, husband and wife, to children, to friends and animals; **vous** is the singular form to indicate politeness, respect or distance. **Vous** referring to one person has any agreeing adjective in the singular

Ma chère Marie, que vous êtes sensible!	My dear Mary, how sensitive you are!

13

2. Emphatic

	1	2	3	
	m. & f.	*m. & f.*	*m.*	*f.*
sg.	moi	toi	lui	elle
pl.	nous	vous	eux	elles

Used for emphasis

| **Toi et moi nous partirons tout** | You and I will leave at once, |
| **de suite, lui suivra plus tard** | he will follow later |

as a co-ordinator

| **Mon père et moi, nous** | My father and I will come |
| **viendrons demain** | tomorrow |

when there is no verb

Qui te l'a dit?	Who told you so?
Toi!	You (did)!
Elle est plus âgée que lui	She is older than he (is)

after prepositions or **comme**

Chez elle	At her house
Il sortit avec eux	He went out with them
Quant à moi	As for me
Je pense comme toi	I agree with you

with verbs of motion to render 'motion to' with **à**

| **Il courut à moi** | He ran to me |
| **Nous sommes allés à elle** | We went to her |

and with **penser à** 'to think of (about)'

| **Je pensais à elle** | I was thinking of her |
| *but* **J'y pensais** | I was thinking of *it* |

with **c'est, c'était**

| **Qui va là? C'est moi** | Who goes there? It's me |

to render the personal idea before a relative clause

| **Toi qui as toujours obéi** | You who always obeyed |
| **à ton père** | your father |

23 The pronoun **y** = **à** or **dans** + a noun which is not a person

| **Je voudrais y penser un peu** | I should like to think |
| (i.e. **à quelque chose**) | about it a bit |

Mon frère joue au tennis	My brother plays tennis
J'y joue aussi	I do, too
Il y a laissé son porte-monnaie	He left his purse there
(i.e. dans cet endroit)	

24 The pronoun **en** = **de** + a noun, whether personal or not

Combien de poires a-t-il?	How many pears has he got?
Il en a deux kilos	He's got two kilos
Voyez-vous venir des agents?	Can you see the police coming?
Non, je n'en vois pas	No, I can't see any
Je vais m'en passer	I will do without it
	(Because se passer **de** quelque-chose)

25 Note the following expressions where the sense of **y** or **en** has faded but where the pronoun is still needed

Il en est de même	It is all the same
Je n'en peux plus	I can't do any more
Je m'y connais	I know a thing or two about that
C'en est fait de moi	I'm done for

26 **On** is more used in French than 'one' is in English

In conversation it is often used where English would use 'we'

| Qu'est-ce qu'on va faire maintenant? | What are we going to do now? |

On has no direct or indirect object form. For these **vous** is used

| On ne perd pas toujours; quelquefois cela vous surprend | One doesn't always lose; sometimes that surprises one |

27 The reflexive pronoun for **on** is **se**; **soi** is used as the emphatic pronoun

| On se rappelle ce qui s'est passé | One remembers what happened |
| On ne devrait pas toujours parler de soi | One shouldn't be always talking about oneself |

Note: **soi** is also the emphatic pronoun for **personne** (nobody); **quiconque** (who(so)ever) and traditionally in

| Chacun pour soi | Each for himself |

28 L'on is sometimes used in written French after **et, ou, que** and **si**

> **Si l'on parle toujours de soi, on**   If you're always talking about
> **risquera de perdre ses amis**   yourself you'll run the risk of
>   losing your friends

29 **Reflexive pronouns**

	1	2	3	
sg.	me, m'	te, t'	se, s'	both direct and indirect
pl.	nous	vous	se, s'	object, e.g. **me** = 'myself' or 'to myself'

These are used with verbs when the action 'reflects back on' the doer
— it affects the subject of the sentence

> **Je me lave avant le petit déjeuner** I wash (myself) before breakfast

30 Verbs which are used reflexively, i.e. with reflexive pronouns, are
more frequent in French than in English. Such verbs should be learnt
with their reflexive pronoun. Thus **se lever**, 'to get up', does not seem
in English to contain any reflexive idea; the reflexive idea in the
French is, however, understandable if we think of the meaning of
lever = 'to raise'. When we raise *ourselves* we get up. Conversely when
we seat *ourselves* we sit down — **s'asseoir**. Sometimes the reflexive
idea is the indirect object — thus **se rappeler quelque chose** (= to
remember something) is really to re-call something *to* oneself; but the
need for, or the explanation of, the reflexive in French is not always
so obvious. Thus, the other word for 'remember' — **se souvenir de
quelque chose**

> **Il s'en souviendra**   He will remember it

31 *Note:* the following uses of the reflexive pronoun

(a) to indicate a part of the body belonging to the subject of the
sentence

> **Marie s'est lavé les cheveux**
> **Marie lui a lavé les cheveux**   Mary has washed her hair

The English is ambiguous; the French is quite clear. The first sentence
means 'Mary has washed the hair belonging *to herself*', i.e. her own
hair. The second one means she has washed someone else's hair.

(b) in expressions where English might use the passive voice

Cela s'entend — That is understood

Le trajet se fit sans incident — The crossing took place without incident

(c) **Il se peut que ...** — It may be that ...

(d) to express the idea of 'one another'

Ils se regardèrent — They looked at each other

This reciprocal idea can be stressed by adding **l'un(e), l'autre** or, if appropriate, **les uns les autres**

(e) in the verb se **tromper** to express the idea of 'wrong' (= mistaken)

Je me suis trompé de route — I took the wrong road

32 Possessive pronouns

		m.		*f.*		
		sg.	*pl.*	*sg.*	*pl.*	
One	1	le mien	les miens	la mienne	les miennes	Agreement
owner	2	le tien	les tiens	la tienne	les tiennes	with the
	3	le sien	les siens	la sienne	les siennes	gender and
						number of
more	1	le nôtre	les nôtres	la nôtre	les nôtres	the noun,
than one	2	le vôtre	les vôtres	la vôtre	les vôtres	not of the
owner	3	le leur	les leurs	la leur	les leurs	owner

Il lui prit la main dans les siennes — He took her hand in his

Prenons ma voiture; il faut garer la vôtre — Let's take my car; we must park yours

Note: a common method of indicating ownership with **être**

C'est à moi — It's mine

Ils sont à moi, ces bijoux — They're mine, those jewels are!

33 Demonstrative pronouns

Simple forms

sg.		*pl.*	
m.	*f.*	*m.*	*f.*
celui	celle	ceux	celles

These forms are not used alone; they are used

(a) with **de** — to indicate ownership

Voici les livres de Marie; ceux de Georges ne sont pas ici	Here are Mary's books; George's aren't here

(b) as an antecedent of a relative pronoun in the sense of 'the one which', 'those which'

Quels gosses? Ceux qui sont sortis tout à l'heure	Which lads? Those who just went out

(c) with **-ci** or **-là** to form

Distinctive forms

celui-ci	**celle-ci**	(this)	**ceux-ci**	**celles-ci**	(these)
celui-là	**celle-là**	(that)	**ceux-là**	**celles-là**	(those)

Simple form when gender is not stressed

ce, c'

ceci

cela (**ça** colloquially)

In English the demonstrative pronoun idea is sometimes expressed by 's only, e.g. 'mine and George's'. This abbreviated usage is not possible in French

De tous les tableaux de l'exposition celui de mon père est le moins coûteux	Of all the pictures in the exhibition, my father's is the least expensive

34   The distinctive forms are already qualified by the addition of **-ci** or **-là**. These additions cannot be used if there is any other qualification

Ces poires sont mûres; celles de mon frère ne le sont pas	These pears are ripe; my brother's aren't
Celui que j'admire n'aurait pas fait cela	The one I admire would not have done that

The distinctive forms are frequently used to render the idea of 'the former', 'the latter'

Tu vois qu'il en y a deux sortes; moi je préfère celle-là mais je crois que tu préfères celle-ci	You see there are two kinds; I prefer the former but I think you prefer the latter

35 The demonstrative pronoun in the simple form is also used to express 'the one (which)'

A cette époque-là j'avais quatre voitures; celle qui me reste maintenant n'est pas celle que je préfère	At that time I had four cars; the one which is now left is not the one I prefer

36 Use of **ce**

(a) with **qui** or **que** to render 'what' in the sense of 'that which'

J'ai ce qu'il faut pour résoudre le problème	I have got what is necessary to solve the problem
Ce qui me plaît, c'est son attitude	What pleases me is his attitude
Tout ce qui reluit n'est pas or	All that glitters is not gold

(b) to emphasize or mark out

C'est à toi que je vais penser	You are the one I shall think about
C'est un peu drôle, un chien qui marche sur les pattes de derrière	A dog that walks on its hind legs is a bit funny

(c) with emphatic pronouns

C'est moi	It is I (me)

37 Indefinite pronouns (negative)

Aucun(e) Nul(le) - used in written French only Pas un(e) Personne Rien	All require ne with the verb if they are used as the subject

Aucun ne doit s'opposer à la volonté du dictateur	No one should oppose the dictator's will
De toutes ces dames pas une n'aura l'honneur de représenter la ville	Of all these ladies not one will have the honour of representing the town
Rien ne fut entendu	Nothing was heard

| Personne ne l'a vu | Nobody saw it |
| Rien de bon | Nothing good |

Note: **rien** sometimes has a positive sense, particularly after **sans, avant de, avant que, pour que**. It will then not have ne with the verb

Avant de rien voir	Before seeing anything
Il se tint là sans rien faire	He stood there without doing anything
Il pleuvait trop pour que j'aie rien vu	It was raining too much for me to have seen anything

38 Indefinite pronouns (positive)

quelqu'un, quelque chose

| Il avait l'air de quelqu'un qui était sur le point de s'évader | He looked like someone about to escape |
| Quelque chose de bon | Something good |

39 l(es) un(s) l(es) autre(s) 'one another'

Note: the use to emphasise the reflexive idea

| Aimez-vous les uns les autres | Love one another |

Note:	**les autres**	the others
	des autres	of the others
	d'autres	others
	d'autrui	of others

	n'importe qui	
or	**qui que ce soit**	whoever
	n'importe quoi	
or	**quoi que ce soit**	whatever

40 Interrogative pronouns

	Persons	*Things*
Subject:	**qui** or **qui est-ce qui?**	**Qu'est-ce qui?**
Object:	**qui** or **qui est-ce que?**	**Qu'est-ce que** or **que?**

| **Qui cherchez vous?** | |
| **Qui est-ce que vous cherchez?** | Who(m) are you looking for? |

Que cherchez-vous?	What are you looking for?
Qu'est-ce que vous cherchez?	
Qui a fait ce bruit?	Who made that noise?
Qui est-ce qui a fait ce bruit?	

After a preposition use **qui** or **quoi**

Par qui a-t-il été fusillé?	By whom was he shot?
De quoi s'agit-il?	What's it about?

41 Where there is a choice or a reference back the interrogative pronoun is

	m.	*f.*
sg.	**lequel?**	**laquelle?**
pl.	**lesquels?**	**lesquelles?**

Elle avait deux filles. Laquelle	She had two daughters. Which of
des deux a-t-il épousée?	the two did he marry?

When used with **de** or **à** the pronoun combines where necessary

Duquel s'est-il servi?	Which one did he use?
Auxquels s'est-elle adressée?	To which people did she speak?

42 Relative pronouns

	Things and persons *m.* and *f.*	Persons	Things
Subject	**qui**		
Object	**que**		
Possessive	**dont**	**de qui**	
With preposition		**qui**	**lequel, laquelle** **lesquels, lesquelles**
with entre and **parmi**			**lesquels, lesquelles**

Le jardin au delà duquel il y a un	The garden beyond which there
ruisseau	is a stream
Les hommes entre lesquels elle	The men between whom she
se trouvait	happened to be

The relative pronoun cannot be omitted in French, as it sometimes is in English

Un homme que je connais	A man I know

Note:

coûte que coûte	cost what it may
advienne que pourra	whatever may happen
une fois que	a time when
un jour que	a day when

but

le jour où	the day when
la fois où	the time when

Adjectives

43 Adjectives agree with their noun in gender and number even if they do not stand immediately next to the noun

| un beau matin | de beaux matins |
| une belle épée | de belles épées |

Ces cerises-ci sont plus blanches que celles-là

44 *But* if the adjective is basically a noun or adverb, no sign of agreement is added

des hommes bien	respectable men *or* men of merit and importance
des rubans cerise	cherry coloured ribbons
des bas marron	chestnut coloured stockings

The same applies to compound adjectives of colour

| des yeux bleu clair, i.e. d'un bleu clair | light blue eyes |
| des chemises rouge foncé | dark red shirts |

45 If the adjective agrees with two nouns one of which is feminine the adjective is in the masculine plural

| Ces femmes et ces hommes sont loyaux | These women and these men are loyal |

46 **Gender.** The feminine form is often made by adding 'e' to the masculine

m.	*f.*	
normal	normale	e.g. **L'Ecole Normale**
blessé	blessée	**une infirmière blessée**

| But *note:* | **feu la reine** | the late queen |
| | or **la feue reine** | |

23

If the masculine form already has an 'e' mute, no addition is made for the feminine

un homme sympathique	a likeable man
une femme sympathique	a likeable woman

47 The following should be noted for their special feminine singular and masculine form in 'l' before a vowel or mute 'h'

sg.			pl.	
m.		*f.*	*m.*	*f.*
beau	bel	belle	beaux	belles
nouveau	nouvel	nouvelle	nouveaux	nouvelles
vieux	vieil	vieille	vieux	vieilles
fou	fol	folle	fous	folles
mou	mol	molle	mous	molles

un bel édifice	a fine building
le nouvel an	the New Year

48 With the following adjectives there is a doubled consonant in the feminine form

m.	*f.*	*m.*	*f.*
bon	bonne	gras	grasse
sot	sotte	gros	grosse
cruel	cruelle	net	nette
		pareil	pareille

49 With the following the final hard 'c' becomes '**que**' in the feminine form

	m.	*f.*	*m.*	*f.*
	turc	turque	public	publique
but	grec	grecque		

50 Other special feminine forms

m.	*f.*		
-x	-se	un mari jaloux	une femme jalouse
-eur	-euse	un discours trompeur	une promesse trompeuse
-teur	-trice	le nerf moteur	une force motrice

24

Exception:	enchanteur	enchanteresse
Note also	frais	fraîche
	blanc	blanche
	sec	sèche

Note: **demi** and **nu** are unchanged before their noun but agree if after it

	nu-tête	la tête nue
	une demi-heure	une heure et demie

51 Plural adjectives usually formed by adding 's' but this is not required if the singular already ends in 's' or 'x'

un homme courageux	des hommes courageux
un chapeau gris	des chapeaux gris

52 Adjectives ending in **-al** make plural in **-aux**

un précepte moral	des préceptes moraux

Exceptions: **fatal, final, natal, naval** which make plural in -s

53 Compound adjectives: if both parts have equal value, both agree

m.	*f.*	
un sourd-muet	une sourde-muette	a deaf mute
des sourds-muets	des sourdes-muettes	deaf mutes

If one part has adverbial value, no agreement of that part is necessary

Dans les rangs elle marchait	In the crocodile she always
toujours l'avant-dernière	walked next to the last

54 Adjectives with varying meaning according to their position

	Before noun	*After noun*
seul	sole, single	alone, solitary
même	same	(it)self
pauvre	poor (sympathetically)	poor (no money)
propre	own	clean
cher	dear (emotionally)	expensive
simple	only, nothing but	simple
dernier	last (of a series)	last (the one just gone)
grand	great	big, tall

ancien	former	old
vrai	real, genuine	true (not fictitious)
C'est la vraie raison		It's the real reason
C'est une anecdote vraie		It's a true tale
Les anciennes élèves		The Old Girls

Note: **autre(s)** as well as meaning 'other' has an emphatic sense with **nous** or **vous**

Nous autres Anglais	We English

55 Position of adjectives before or after noun

Rules are difficult to lay down as French writers consider not only custom but also stress, variety, degree of intensity and euphony, but the general practice is

Before

1. possessives, demonstratives, numbers

mon habit	**les deux sœurs**
cette rose	**la troisième année**
Except in title	**Charles premier**

2. the indefinite **n'importe quel** (see paragraph 58)

3. **beau, bon, court, gros, haut, jeune, joli, sot, vaste, vilain, mauvais, long, petit, vieux, méchant**

After

1. adjectives denoting colour, nationality, religion

un imperméable bleu	a blue raincoat
l'église catholique	the Catholic church
un soldat grec	a Greek soldier

2. participles used as adjectives

un enfant gâté	a spoilt child
une histoire touchante	a moving story

3. if qualified by an adverb or phrase longer than one or two syllables

un sourire beau comme l'aurore	a smile as beautiful as dawn
un argument entièrement faux	an entirely false argument
une maison haute de 10 mètres	a house ten metres high
but: **un très beau sourire**	
une assez courte rue	
un si joli visage	

4. This same idea – i.e. that of length – generally brings adjectives which are longer than their noun after it

une plainte acrimonieuse	a bitter complaint
le cadre professionnel	the professional cadre

56 Adjectives of quantity

Nul, nulle, aucun, aucune, (= no) are used in the singular only, and if the noun they qualify is the subject or object of the sentence require ne with the verb

Je n'ai vu aucune trace de cet homme	I have seen no sign of that man
Nulle femme ne doit y entrer	No woman may go in

Certain(e)(s), quelque(s), plusieurs (= 'several', always plural) **maint(e)(s)** (= 'many a', in the singular) **chaque, tout(e)(s) tous**

Maint navire a sombré là	Many a ship has foundered there

57 Other expressions of quantity

beaucoup de ⎫		**tant de**	so many
pas mal de ⎬ many		**autant de**	as many
peu de ⎭ few		**assez de**	enough

The de must be used if a noun follows

beaucoup de gens	many people
assez de vin	enough wine
tant de journaux	so many newspapers

58 Indeterminate expressions and indefinite adjectives

n'importe quel(le)(s) before the noun

On le trouve dans n'importe quel journal	You can find it in any newspaper you like

quelconque(s) after the noun, usually with a slightly derogatory sense

Il est arrivé dans une voiture quelconque	He came in some sort of car or other

quel(le)(s) que . . . . with the verb in the subjunctive

quels que soient les résultats . . .	whatever the results may be . . .

27

59 Comparison

ascending	e.g. useful	more useful	the most useful
	utile(s)	plus utile(s)	le (la, les) plus utile(s)
descending	e.g. useful	less useful	the least useful
	utile(s)	moins utile(s)	le (la, les) moins utile(s)

Il est plus laid que son frère	He is uglier than his brother
Il est le plus laid de tous	He is the ugliest of the lot
Nous serons moins contents que nos voisins	We shall be less satisfied than our neighbours
Ce sont les plus belles jeunes filles de la ville	They are the most beautiful girls in the town

60 Equal comparison

aussi . . . . que	as . . . . as
Elle est aussi gentille que jolie	She's as nice as she is pretty
Il était aussi grand que son oncle	He was as tall as his uncle

61 Note the use of **que** = than

Notre chien est plus grand que le vôtre	Our dog is bigger than yours

and the need for **ne** in a following clause

Elle est plus heureuse qu'elle ne l'était autrefois	She is happier than she used to be

62 Irregular comparisons

good	better	best
bon(ne)(s)	meilleur(e)(s)	le (la, les) meilleur(e)(s)
bad	worse	worst
mauvais(e)(s)	pire(s)	le (la, les) pire(s)
	or plus mauvais(e)(s)	or le (la, les) plus mauvais(e)(s)
petit(e)(s)	plus petit(e)(s)	le (la, les) plus petit(e)(s)
	or moindre(s)	

Note:

(a) **pis** when not referring to a specific noun

tant pis	so much the worse

(b) the false superlative

une femme des plus charmantes	a most charming woman
un cheval des plus fringants	a most lively horse

another way of rendering it – particularly without a noun

Elle est extrêmement belle	She is most beautiful

63 Interrogative and exclamatory adjectives

	m.	*f.*
sg.	**quel**	**quelle**
pl.	**quels**	**quelles**

Quel âge as-tu?	How old are you?
Quelle bêtise!	What a stupid thing!
Quel dommage!	What a pity!

Adverbs

64 **Position** In English an adverb may be found between the subject and the verb. This is not so in French. If the verb is in a simple tense, the adverb will follow the verb

    Il joue souvent le soir   He often plays in the evening

If the verb is in a compound tense the adverb will generally follow the auxiliary verb unless the adverb is long; in that case it will follow the past participle

    Il a souvent manqué ce train   He has often missed this train
    Il a parlé continuellement   He went on talking

The French have a dislike of an abrupt ending to a sentence; it is to avoid this that an adverb will frequently come between the auxiliary verb and the past participle, e.g.

    Vous avez mal répondu
    Il est bien arrivé

Sometimes the position is a matter of taste and meaning. Thus
Il est sorti vite and **Il est vite sorti** are both possible; the latter emphasizes the speed of going out

65 **Formation** Most simple adverbs of time, place and quantity are derived from Latin, e.g. **bien, mal, puis, bientôt, ensemble, parfois, souvent, mieux.**
Beware of the English 'better' which is used both as an adjective and an adverb

    C'est un meilleur artiste que son   He is a better artist than his
    frère   brother
    Il joue mieux que son frère   He plays better than his brother

66 Most adverbs of manner are formed by adding **-ment** to the feminine form of the adjective

	Adjective		*Adverb*	
m.	*f.*			
franc	**franche**	**franchement**	freely	

doux	douce	doucement	gently
long	longue	longuement	at great length
		(long = a long time =	
		longtemps)	

67 If the feminine form of the adjective ends in a stressed vowel the 'e' of the feminine form is usually omitted

vrai	vraie	vraiment	truly

Sometimes the lost 'e' is represented by ˆ as in

	dûment	duly
	continûment	continuously
but	gaiement	
and	gaîment are both found	

68 If the adjective has the ending -**ant** or -**ent** the adverb is formed in -**amment** or -**emment** as in

Adjective	*Adverb*
courant	couramment
élégant	élégamment
galant	galamment
prudent	prudemment

69 Note the é in

aveugle	aveuglément
obscure	obscurément
profond	profondément
précis	précisément
énorme	énormément

70 And the exceptional

gentil	gentiment
traître	traîtreusement

71 Adjectives used adverbially in the following expressions

parler haut	to speak loud
parler bas	to speak in a low voice

31

coûter cher	to be dear (cost)
chanter fort	to sing loud
chanter faux	to sing off key
sentir bon	to smell good
pousser dru	to grow thick and fast

and the alliterative mixture

bel et bien	fairly and squarely

Particular uses of other common adverbs

72   **assez** = 'fairly' or 'enough'

Son père était assez riche	His father was fairly rich
Son père était assez riche pour lui acheter l'appartement	His father was *rich enough* to buy the flat for him

(Note different word order in English)

73   **trop** = 'too' (qualifying an adjective)

Sa mère était trop faible pour se hâter	His mother was too weak to hurry

('too' = 'also' is rendered by **aussi**)

74   **comme** = 'how' (in exclamations). Note the word order

Comme elle est charmante!	How charming she is!
also: **Qu'elle est charmante!**	

'how' in questions is **comment**

Comment peut-on l'accuser?	How can one accuse him?

75   **si** = 'so' or 'such a' (qualifying an adjective)

Il est si jeune	He is so young
Ils ont fait un si beau jardin	They have made such a beautiful garden

76   **donc** = 'so' in the explanatory sense

Je suis donc rentré chez moi	And so I went home

donc with an imperative gives an emphatic or pleading note

Dites-moi donc!	Do tell me!

77 **plus** = '(the) more' in comparisons

Il est plus soigneux que son frère	He is more careful than his brother
Plus je connais les hommes, plus j'aime les bêtes	The more I know men, the more I like animals

'more than' followed by a number is **plus de**

Il possédait plus de cent hectares	He owned more than a hundred hectares

For 'more' when there is no comparison use **davantage**

Il faut qu'il s'applique davantage	He must put more into his work

78 **alors** =

1. 'then' (at that time)

On avait alors peu d'argent	We had little money then

2. in conversation, 'well then' often with an expletive

Zut alors!	**Eh bien alors!**

79 **puis** = 'then' in the sense of 'the next thing that happened'. It comes as first idea in the clause

Il monta sur l'échafaud, pria quelques secondes, puis il fit signe au bourreau	He climbed on to the scaffold, prayed for a few seconds, then signalled to the executioner

80 **bientôt** = 'soon'

but   very soon = **très tôt**
         sooner = **plus tôt**
         too soon = **trop tôt**

81 **encore** =

1. 'yet'

Elle n'a pas encore passé son examen	She hasn't passed her exam yet

2. 'still'

Il est encore là	He is still there

82 **toujours** =
1. 'always'
   Elle paraît toujours être heureuse She always seems to be happy

2. 'still'
   La neige tombait toujours The snow was still falling

83 **bien** =
1. 'well'
   Eh bien! C'est toi Well! It's you
   Elle a bien travaillé She worked well

2. 'very' + adjective
   Je suis bien content I am very satisfied

3. almost adjectival = 'all right'
   On est bien ici We're comfortable here

4. 'indeed'
   Je lui ai bien dit de ranger ses affaires I did indeed tell him to tidy his belongings

84 **tant** = 'so much', 'so many'
   tant mieux so much the better
   tant pis so much the worse

   J'ai eu tant d'ennuis I've had so much trouble
   (also in conversation **tellement de**)

Negatives

85 With verbs

1. Not	ne . . . pas	
2. Not at all	ne . . . point	
3. Never	ne . . . jamais	
4. No more, no longer	ne . . . plus	
5. Nothing	ne . . . rien	Rien ne . .
6. Nobody	ne . . . personne	Personne ne . .
7. Only	ne . . . que	
8. Hardly	ne . . . guère	
9. Neither . . . nor	ni. . . . ni. . . . (ne)	

Il ne dit jamais de telles choses	He never says things like that
Elle n'a plus d'argent	She no longer has any money
Ça ne fait rien	It doesn't matter

In compound tenses the above negatives (except **ne . . . personne**) enclose the auxiliary verb

Je ne l'ai jamais vu	I have never seen him
Je n'ai vu personne	I saw nobody
Ni l'un ni l'autre	Neither one nor the other
Ni vous ni lui n'étiez là	Neither you nor he were there

Of course when the **personne** or **rien** comes first as subject of the sentence this cannot apply

Rien n'a marché aujourd'hui	Nothing went well today

Before an infinitive nos. 1 to 5 above come together

Prière de ne pas marcher sur le gazon	Please don't walk on the grass

The **pas** is sometimes omitted with **pouvoir, cesser, oser, savoir**

La patronne n'osa lui refuser une chambre	The manageress didn't dare to refuse him a room

35

Note: The use of ne in subordinate clauses where no negative is implied in the sense

> **Elle marche moins facilement**   She walks less easily than I
> **que je ne pensais**   thought

    (a) After verbs of fearing and **à moins que**

> **On craint qu'il ne vienne**   They fear he will come
> (cf. **On craint qu'il ne vienne pas**   They fear he won't come)
> **A moins qu'il ne soit là** ....   Unless he is there

The **ne** is not used after a verb of fearing if that verb is in the negative or interrogative form (see paragraph 158, *Note*)

    (b) The use of **non** or **pas** to negative an expression when there is no verb

> **Qui est-ce qui l'a fait? Pas moi**   Who did it? Not me
> **Un passage à niveau non gardé**   An unattended level crossing
> **Pas de bande**   No white lines (traffic notice)

Prepositions

The following expressions containing prepositions are listed because the usage is different from the corresponding English

87 **A, à**

(a) The descriptive **à** (English 'with')

La fille aux cheveux roux	The girl with red hair
L'homme au nez rouge	The man with the red nose

(b) Time of the clock

à midi	at twelve o'clock
à deux heures	at two o'clock

(c) In the style of

Un jardin à l'anglaise	An English style garden

(d) Church festivals

à Noël	at Christmas
à la Pentecôte	at Whitsuntide

(e) **à la main**   in (his) hand
      à la campagne   in the country
      (but **en ville**)
      au ciel   in heaven
      (but **en enfer**)
      au dix-huitième siècle   in the eighteenth century
      au printemps   in the spring
      (but **en hiver** etc.)
      à la mode   in the manner, fashion
      à mon avis   in my opinion
      à sa mine   by his expression
      à cheval   on horseback
      peu à peu   gradually, little by little
      côte à côte   side by side

(Je veux acheter) à boire et à manger	something to eat and drink
Il $\left\{\begin{array}{l}\text{reproche}\\ \text{ressemble}\\ \text{résiste}\end{array}\right\}$ à son père	He $\left\{\begin{array}{l}\text{reproaches}\\ \text{looks like}\\ \text{resists}\end{array}\right\}$ his father
jouer au golf (games)	to play golf
but jouer du violon (musical instruments)	to play the violin

(f) The idea of removal *from* is rendered by à with the following verbs: **prendre, voler, cacher, acheter, emprunter**

Il cacha le lapin à son père	He hid the rabbit from his father

(g) With the following verbs the **personal** object has à: **commander, conseiller, demander, défendre** (forbid), **dire, permettre, persuader, promettre,** . . . and a following infinitive is preceded by **de**

Il lui demanda de mettre la lettre à la poste	He asked him to post the letter
Il dit au garçon de lui apporter l'addition	He told the waiter to bring him the bill

88 De

Le train de Marseille	The train to Marseilles (also from Marseilles)
Je suis sorti de chez moi	I left home
Nous venons de le quitter	We have just left him
De loin	From afar
(Au loin)	(In the distance)
Plus de quatre	More than four
Moins de huit	Less than eight
C'est à toi de payer	It's your turn to pay
De ce côté	On this side
Une tasse de thé	A cup of tea
(une tasse à thé)	(a tea cup)
Il est de service	He's on duty
Je suis de retour	I'm back
De cette façon (manière)	In this way (manner)
Quelque chose de bon	Something good

Rien de certain	Nothing certain
Personne d'autre	No one else
S'éloigner de ⎫ quelqu'un	To go away from ⎫ someone
S'approcher de ⎭	To approach ⎭

89 En

'In' with dates	en 1066
with feminine countries	en Allemagne
provinces	en Provence
languages	en français
months	en décembre
by car	en voiture, en auto
by plane	en avion
to believe in God	croire en Dieu
to treat as a brother	traiter en frère
to act like a friend	agir en ami
The prince changed into a frog	Le prince se changea en grenouille

Note: 'in' with expressions of time

Il le fera en deux heures
Il le fera dans deux heures   He will do it in two hours

In the first sentence the French means he will take two hours to do it. In the second it means he will tackle it two hours from now. Put simply, in time expressions 'in' is rendered by **'en'** for duration and by **'dans'** for point of time.

90 Par

par exemple	for example
par monts et par vaux	o'er hill and dale
par conséquent	in consequence
par tête	per head
trois fois par an	three times a year
par un jour de pluie	on a rainy day
par un temps comme ça	in weather like that

91 Depuis

Depuis Puget jusqu'à Digne le terrain devient de plus en plus sauvage — From Puget to Digne the country gets wilder and wilder

Nous habitons Versailles depuis dix ans — We've been living in Versailles for ten years

92 Pour

Pour avoir passé si peu de temps en France vous parlez assez bien le français — Although you have spent so short a time in France you speak French quite well.

cinq pour cent — 5%

Pour vingt francs s'il vous plaît — 20 francs worth (of petrol) please

93 Sous

Sous le règne de Louis XIV — In Louis XIV's reign

94 Sur

deux sur trois — two out of three

sur ces entrefaites — in the meantime

sur le champ — at once, on the spot

Verbs

95 For convenience, verbs are here divided into five groups.

     I. auxiliary verbs: **être** and **avoir**
    II. verbs with infinitive in **-er**   e.g. **passer**
   III. verbs with infinitive in **-ir**   e.g. **blanchir**
   IV. verbs with infinitive in **-re**   e.g. **rendre**
    V. other verbs including irregular ones

96 Tenses are of two kinds: simple and compound. Simple are those where the verb consists of one word, compound are those consisting of an auxiliary verb and a past participle. Simple tenses are formed by adding specific endings to a verb stem; the stem is, usually but not always, what remains when the distinctive ending of the infinitive is removed.

    Thus **passer:**   stem   **pass-**
           rendre: stem   **rend-**
    but **blanchir** has both **blanch-** and **blanchiss-** as stem

In some tenses or for some persons the verb endings are the same for verbs of all groups. These common endings are:

97 **Simple tenses**

Pr. indic.	1p. *pl.* -ons	2p. *pl.* -ez	3p. *pl.* -ent		

Exceptions	être	avoir	faire	dire	aller
	nous sommes	-	-	-	-
	vous êtes	-	vous faites	vous dites	-
	ils sont	ils ont	ils font	-	ils vont

	1p. *sg.*	2p. *sg.*	3p. *sg.*	1p. *pl.*	2p. *pl.*	3p. *pl.*
Future	-rai	-ras	-ra	-rons	-rez	-ront
Imperfect	-ais	-ais	-ait	-ions	-iez	-aient
Conditional	-rais	-rais	-rait	-rions	-riez	-raient

98 Compound tenses

Perfect (passé composé): Present tense of **avoir** or, if appropriate, of **être** + past participle

Pluperfect: Imperfect tense of **avoir** or, if appropriate, of **être** + past participle

Passé antérieur: Passé simple of **avoir** or, if appropriate, of **être** + past participle

99 The use of avoir and être as *auxiliary verbs*

1. Most verbs use **avoir**:

   L'ayant vu de loin,   Having seen him from afar,
   j'ai décidé de le suivre   I decided to follow him

2. Reflexive verbs use **être**:

   M'étant rappelé l'heure de mon   Remembering the time of my
   train, je me suis hâté de sortir   train, I hastened to go out

3. Most intransitive verbs of motion use **être**; the commonest are:
   aller, arriver, partir, venir
   Ils sont arrivés ce matin   They arrived this morning

4. **Rester** uses **être**:
   Elle était restée là   She had remained there

5. Intransitive verbs indicating change of state use **être**:
   naître, mourir, décéder, devenir, éclore

6. With **descendre, monter, sortir,** the auxiliary to be used will depend on the meaning of the verb. Thus if the verb is used intransitively it will use **être**; if transitively, **avoir**

   Nous sommes montés au 4ᵉ étage We climbed to the fourth floor
   Le porteur a monté les bagages The porter has brought up the luggage

   Il est sorti à huit heures He went out at 8 o'clock
   Il a sorti son stylo He pulled out his fountain pen
   Nous étions descendus par We had come down the stairs
   l'escalier pendant que l'ascenseur whilst the lift was going up
   montait
   Nous avions descendu les colis We had brought the parcels down

100 *Note:* (a) In categories 3, 4, 5, 6 above when **être** is used the past participle must agree with the subject

(b) When **avoir** is used the past participle agrees with the *preceding* direct object
Voici les roses que j'ai cueillies
Où est ta mère?   Je ne l'ai pas vue

(c) With reflexive verbs the past participle also agrees with the preceding direct object
Elle s'est lavée
But   **Elle s'est lavé les mains** because the reflexive se is an *indirect* object in this sentence (the hands belonging *to herself*)

Group I

101   Auxiliary verb: **avoir**

| Infinitive: | avoir | Present participle: | ayant |
| Imperative: | aie, ayons, ayez! | Past participle: | eu |

Simple Tenses

	Indicative	Subjunctive
Present	j'ai, tu as, il a nous avons, vous avez, ils ont	j'aie, tu aies, il ait, nous ayons, vous ayez, ils aient
Future	j'aurai, tu auras, il aura nous aurons, vous aurez, ils auront	
Imperfect	j'avais, tu avais, il avait nous avions, vous aviez, ils avaient	j'eusse, tu eusses, il eût nous eussions, vous eussiez ils eussent
Conditional	j'aurais, tu aurais, il aurait, nous aurions, vous auriez, ils auraient	
Passé simple	j'eus, tu eus, il eut, nous eûmes, vous eûtes, ils eurent	

Compound tenses

Indicative	Subjunctive
Perfect (passé composé)	
j'ai eu, tu as eu, etc.	j'aie eu, tu aies eu, il ait eu etc.
Pluperfect	
j'avais eu, tu avais eu, etc.	j'eusse eu, tu eusses eu, il eût eu, etc.
Passé antérieur	
J'eus eu, tu eus eu, il eut eu, etc.	–

102 Idiomatic uses of **avoir**

avoir peur	to be afraid
avoir faim (soif)	to be hungry (thirsty)
avoir besoin de quelque chose	to need something
avoir froid (chaud)	to be cold (hot) – of persons only*
avoir l'air (malheureux)	to look (unhappy)
avoir envie de	to wish
avoir lieu	to take place
avoir raison (tort)	to be right (wrong)

* For weather see para 130

103 Auxiliary verb: **être**

Infinitive:	être	Present participle:	étant
Imperative:	sois, soyons, soyez!	Past participle:	été

Simple tenses

	Indicative	Subjunctive
Present	je suis, tu es, il est, nous sommes, vous êtes, ils sont	je sois, tu sois, il soit, nous soyons, vous soyez, ils soient
Future	je serai, tu seras, il sera, nous serons, vous serez, ils seront	–
Imperfect	j'étais, tu étais, il était, nous étions, vous étiez, ils étaient	je fusse, tu fusses, il fût, nous fussions, vous fussiez, ils fussent

Conditional	je serais, tu serais, il serait,	–
	nous serions, vous seriez,	
	ils seraient	

Passé simple	je fus, tu fus, il fut,	–
	nous fûmes, vous fûtes,	
	ils furent	

Compound tenses

Perfect (passé composé)
j'ai été, tu as été, il a été, etc.

j'aie été, tu aies été,
il ait été, etc.

Pluperfect
j'avais été, tu avais été, il avait été,
etc.

j'eusse été, tu eusses été,
il eût été, etc.

Passé antérieur
j'eus été, tu eus été, il eut été, etc. –

104 Group II

Infinitive:	passer	Present participle:	passant
Imperative:	passe, passons,	Past participle:	passé
	passez!		

Simple tenses

	Indicative	**Subjunctive**
Present	je passe, tu passes, il passe,	je passe, tu passes, il passe,
	nous passons, vous passez,	nous passions, vous passiez,
	ils passent	ils passent
Future	je passerai, tu passeras,	–
	il passera	
	nous passerons, vous passerez	
	ils passeront	
Imperfect	je passais, tu passais,	je passasse, tu passasses,
	il passait,	il passât
	nous passions, vous passiez,	nous passassions, vous
	ils passaient	passassiez, ils passassent

Conditional	je passerais, tu passerais,	–
	il passerait,	
	nous passerions, vous passeriez,	
	ils passeraient	

Passé simple	je passai, tu passas, il passa	–
	nous passâmes, vous passâtes,	
	ils passèrent	

Compound tenses

Perfect (passé composé)

j'ai passé, tu as passé, il a passé, etc.   j'aie passé, tu aies passé,
il ait passé, etc.

Pluperfect

j'avais passé, tu avais passé,   j'eusse passé, tu eusses
il avait passé, etc.   passé, il eût passé, etc.

Passé antérieur

j'eus passé, tu eus passé, il eut passé,   –
etc.

105 **-er** verbs which differ from the verbs in Group II in some respects.

1. doubling the consonant in parts of the present tense before a mute e

jeter and its compounds	**appeler**
je jette	j'appelle
tu jettes	tu appelles
il jette	il appelle
nous jetons	nous appelons
vous jetez	vous appelez
ils jettent	ils appellent

2. using the grave accent before a mute **e**

lever and its compounds		**semer**	
je lève	also: acheter	je sème	and in the future
tu lèves	geler	tu sèmes	je sèmerai etc.
il lève		il sème	
nous levons		nous semons	
vous levez		vous semez	
ils lèvent		ils sèment	

3. using e after **g** or cedilla under **c** to keep the stem sound soft.

Present	*Imperative*	*Passé simple*
nous bougeons, lançons	je bougeais, etc.	je bougeai
	je lançais	je lançai

Present participles
bougeant, lançant

4. changing acute to grave before a mute e

je préfère	also: compléter,	*but note:* the future tense
tu préfères	refléter	je préférerai
il préfère	espérer	
nous préférons		
vous préférez		
ils préfèrent		

5. verbs in **-yer**, change the **y** to **i** before mute e

j'appuie	but verbs in **-ayer**
tu appuies	e.g. balayer, payer, may change the 'y' to 'i'
il appuie	or may retain the 'y' before a mute 'e'
nous appuyons	
vous appuyez	
ils appuient	

6. **envoyer** in future and conditional: j'enverrai, j'enverrais

106 Group III

Infinitive:	finir	Present participle:	finissant
Imperative:	finis, finissons, finissez!	Past participle:	fini

Simple tenses

	Indicative	Subjunctive
Present	je finis, tu finis, il finit	je finisse, tu finisses, il finisse,
	nous finissons, vous finissez, ils finissent	nous finissions, vous finissiez, ils finissent
Future	je finirai, tu finiras, il finira, nous finirons, vous finirez, ils finiront	—

Imperfect	je finissais, tu finissais, il finissait nous finissions, vous finissiez, ils finissaient		je finisse, tu finisses, il finît, nous finissions, vous finissiez, ils finissent
Conditional	je finirais, tu finirais, il finirait nous finirions, vous finiriez, ils finiraient		–
Passé simple	je finis, tu finis, il finit, nous finîmes, vous finîtes, ils finirent		–

Compound tenses

Perfect (passé composé)

j'ai fini, tu as fini, il a fini, etc.   j'aie fini, tu aies fini, il ait fini, etc.

Pluperfect

j'avais fini, tu avais fini, il avait fini, etc.   j'eusse fini, tu eusses fini, il eût fini, etc.

Passé antérieur

j'eus fini, tu eus fini, il eut fini, etc.   –

107 There are some **-ir** verbs which differ from the Group III conjugation in some respects. See the following in Group V:

accueillir	cueillir	haïr	revenir
acquérir	découvrir	mourir	sentir
appartenir	devenir	obtenir	servir
assaillir	dormir	offrir	souffrir
bouillir	s'endormir	partir	se souvenir
convenir	s'enfuir	parvenir	tenir
courir	faillir	prévenir	venir
couvrir	fuir	recueillir	vêtir

108 Group IV

Infinitive:	rendre	Present participle:	rendant
Imperative:	rends, rendons, rendez!	Past participle:	rendu

Simple tenses

	Indicative	Subjunctive
Present	je rends, tu rends, il rend,	je rende, tu rendes, il rende,
	nous rendons, vous rendez, ils rendent	nous rendions, vous rendiez, ils rendent
Future	je rendrai, tu rendras, il rendra, nous rendrons, vous rendrez, ils rendront	
Imperfect	je rendais, tu rendais, il rendait, nous rendions, vous rendiez, ils rendaient	je rendisse, tu rendisses, il rendît nous rendissions, vous rendissiez, ils rendissent
Conditional	je rendrais, tu rendrais, ils rendrait nous rendrions, vous rendriez, ils rendraient	
Passé simple	je rendis, tu rendis, il rendit, nous rendîmes, vous rendîtes, ils rendirent	

Compound tenses

Perfect (passé composé)

j'ai rendu, tu as rendu, il a rendu, etc.	j'aie rendu, tu aies rendu, il ait rendu, etc.

Pluperfect

j'avais rendu, tu avais rendu, il avait rendu, etc.	j'eusse rendu, tu eusses rendu, il eût rendu, etc.

Passé antérieur

j'eus rendu, tu eus rendu, il eut rendu, etc.	—

49

109 There are some **-re** verbs which differ from the Group IV conjugation in some respects. See the following in Group V:

abattre	convaincre	luire	résoudre
admettre	craindre	maudire	rire
apparaître	croire	moudre	rompre
apprendre	croître	paraître	sourire
battre	détruire	peindre	suffire
boire	dire	permettre	suivre
combattre	disparaître	plaire	surprendre
comprendre	écrire	poursuivre	survivre
conclure	faire	prendre	se taire
conduire	instruire	produire	vaincre
confire	interrompre	promettre	vivre
connaître	joindre	reconnaître	
construire	lire	reprendre	

110 Group V

Other verbs including irregular ones

In the lists on the following pages the parts of verbs given are the minimum. Thus of the future, perfect, and imperfect tenses only the first person is given, the endings of these tenses being regular.

Nor is any part of the conditional, pluperfect and passé antérieur tenses given. The conditional can be formed, once the future stem is known and the formation of the pluperfect and passé antérieur can be deduced from the perfect.

Only the first person of the passé simple is given; the rest of the endings follow the appropriate pattern:

-ai	-is	-us
-as	-is	-us
-a	-it	-ut
-âmes	-îmes	-ûmes
-âtes	-îtes	-ûtes
-èrent	-irent	-urent

INFINITIVE	PRES. PARTIC.	PRES. INDIC.	PRES. SUBJUN.	FUTURE	IMPERFECT	PASSÉ SIMPLE	PERFECT
111							
abattre — like battre							
accueillir — like cueillir							
acquérir	acquérant	j'acquiers tu acquiers il acquiert ns. acquérons vs. acquérez ils acquièrent	acquière acquières acquière acquérions acquériez acquièrent	acquerrai	acquérais	acquis	j'ai acquis
admettre — like mettre							
aller	allant	je vais tu vas il va ns. allons vs. allez ils vont	aille ailles aille allions alliez aillent	irai	allais	allai	je suis allé

INFINITIVE	PRES. PARTIC.	PRES. INDIC.	PRES. SUBJUN.	FUTURE	IMPERFECT	PASSÉ SIMPLE	PERFECT
apparaître — like connaître							
appartenir — like tenir							
apercevoir — like recevoir							
apprendre — like prendre							
assaillir	assaillant	j'assaille tu assailles il assaille ns. assaillons vs. assaillez ils assaillent	assaille assailles assaille assaillions assailliez assaillent	assaillirai	assaillais	assaillis	j'ai assailli
s'asseoir	s'asseyant	je m'assieds tu t'assieds il s'assied ns. ns. asseyons vs. vs. asseyez ils s'asseyent	m'asseye t'asseyes s'asseye ns. asseyions vs. asseyiez s'asseyent	m'assiérai	m'asseyais	m'assis	je me suis assis

52

112

battre	battant	je bats tu bats il bat ns. battons vs. battez ils battent	batte battes batte battions battiez battent	battrai	battais	battis	j'ai battu
boire	buvant	je bois tu bois il boit ns. buvons vs. buvez ils boivent	boive boives boive buvions buviez boivent	boirai	buvais	bus	j'ai bu
bouillir	bouillant	je bous tu bous il bout ns. bouillons vs. bouillez ils bouillent	bouille bouilles bouille bouillions bouilliez bouillent	bouillirai	bouillais	bouillis	j'ai bouilli

113

combattre —
like battre

INFINITIVE	PRES. PARTIC.	PRES. INDIC.	PRES. SUBJUN.	FUTURE	IMPERFECT	PASSÉ SIMPLE	PERFECT
comprendre — like prendre							
conclure	concluant	je conclus tu conclus il conclut ns. concluons vs. concluez ils concluent	conclue conclues conclue concluions concluiez concluent	conclurai	concluais	conclus	j'ai conclu
conduire	conduisant	je conduis tu conduis il conduit ns. conduisons vs. conduisez ils conduisent	conduise conduises conduise conduisions conduisiez conduisent	conduirai	conduisais	conduisis	j'ai conduit
connaître	connaissant	je connais tu connais il connaît ns. connaissons vs. connaissez ils connaissent	connaisse connaisses connaisse connaissions connaissiez connaissent	connaîtrai	connaissais	connus	j'ai connu

construire –
like conduire
convaincre –
like vaincre

	Participe	Présent	Subjonctif	Futur	Imparfait	Passé simple	Passé composé
coudre	cousant	je couds tu couds il coud ns. cousons vs. cousez ils cousent	couse couses couse cousions cousiez cousent	coudrai	cousais	cousis	j'ai cousu
courir	courant	je cours tu cours il court ns. courons vs. courez ils courent	coure coures coure courions couriez courent	courrai	courais	courus	j'ai couru
couvrir – like ouvrir							
craindre	craignant	je crains tu crains il craint ns. craignons vs. craignez ils craignent	craigne craignes craigne craignions craigniez craignent	craindrai	craignais	craignis	j'ai craint

INFINITIVE	PRES. PARTIC.	PRES. INDIC.	PRES. SUBJUN.	FUTURE	IMPERFECT	PASSÉ SIMPLE	PERFECT
croire	croyant	je crois tu crois il croit ns. croyons vs. croyez ils croient	croie croies croie croyions croyiez croient	croirai	croyais	crus	j'ai cru
croître	croissant	je croîs tu croîs il croît ns. croissons vs. croissez ils croissent	croisse croisses croisse croissions croissiez croissent	croîtrai	croissais	crûs	j'ai crû
cueillir	cueillant	je cueille tu cueilles il cueille ns. cueillions vs. cueillez ils cueillent	cueille cueilles cueille cueillions cueilliez cueillent	cueillerai	cueillais	cueillis	j'ai cueilli

114

cuire –
like conduire

découvrir –
like couvrir

détruire –
like conduire

devenir –
like venir

devoir	devant	je dois tu dois il doit ns. devons vs. devez ils doivent	doive doives doive devions deviez doivent	devrai	devais	dus	j'ai dû (^ disappears if feminine)
dire	disant	je dis tu dis il dit ns. disons vs. dites ils disent	dise dises dise disions disiez disent	dirai	disais	dis	j'ai dit

INFINITIVE	PRES. PARTIC.	PRES. INDIC.	PRES. SUBJUN.	FUTURE	IMPERFECT	PASSE SIMPLE	PERFECT
disparaître – like connaître							
dormir	dormant	je dors tu dors il dort ns. dormons vs. dormez ils dorment	dorme dormes dorme dormions dormiez dorment	dormirai	dormais	dormis	j'ai dormi
115							
écrire	écrivant	j'écris tu écris il écrit ns. écrivons ns. écrivez ils écrivent	écrive écrives écrive écrivions écriviez écrivent	écrirai	écrivais	écrivis	j'ai écrit
s'endormir – like dormir							
s'enfuir – like fuir							

envoyer	envoyant	j'envoie tu envoies il envoie ns. envoyons vs. envoyez ils envoient	envoie envoies envoie envoyions envoyiez envoient	enverrai	envoyais	envoyai	j'ai envoyé

éteindre –
like craindre

116

faillir	(faillant)	je (faux) tu (faux) il (faut) ns. (faillons) vs. (faillez) ils (faillent)	(faille) (failles) (faille) (faillions) (failliez) (faillent)	faillirai	(il faillait)	faillis	j'ai failli
faire	faisant	je fais tu fais il fait ns. faisons vs. faites ils font	fasse fasses fasse fassions fassiez fassent	ferai	faisais	fis	j'ai fait

INFINITIVE	PRES. PARTIC.	PRES. INDIC.	PRES. SUBJUN.	FUTURE	IMPERFECT	PASSÉ SIMPLE	PERFECT
falloir		il faut	il faille	il faudra	il fallait	il fallut	il a fallu
fuir	fuyant	je fuis	fuie	fuirai	fuyais	fuis	j'ai fui
		tu fuis	fuies				
		il fuit	fuie				
		ns. fuyons	fuyions				
		vs. fuyez	fuyiez				
		ils fuient	fuyent				
117							
haïr	haïssant	je hais	haïsse	haïrai	haïssais	haïs	j'ai haï
		tu hais	haïsses				
		il hait	haïsse				
		ns. haïssons	haïssions				
		vs. haïssez	haïssiez				
		ils haïssent	haïssent				

instruire –
like conduire

interrompre –
like rompre

joindre –
like craindre

lire	lisant	je lis tu lis il lit ns. lisons vs. lisez ils lisent	lise lises lise lisions lisiez lisent	lirai	lisais	lus	j'ai lu
luire	luisant	je luis tu luis il luit ns. luisons vs. luisez ils luisent	luise luises luise luisions luisiez luisent	luirai	luisais	luisis	j'ai lui

118

maudire	maudissant	je maudis tu maudis il maudit ns. maudissons vs. maudissez ils maudissent	maudisse maudisses maudisse maudissions maudissiez maudissent	maudirai	maudissais	maudis	j'ai maudit

61

INFINITIVE	PRES. PARTIC.	PRES. INDIC.	PRES. SUBJUN.	FUTURE	IMPERFECT	PASSÉ SIMPLE	PERFECT
mentir – like dormir							
mettre	mettant	je mets tu mets il met ns. mettons vs. mettez ils mettent	mette mettes mette mettions mettiez mettent	mettrai	mettais	mis	j'ai mis
moudre	moulant	je mouds tu mouds il moud ns. moulons vs. moulez ils moulent	moule moules moule moulions mouliez moulent	moudrai	moulais	moulus	j'ai moulu
mourir	mourant	je meurs tu meurs il meurt ns. mourons vs. mourez ils meurent	meure meures meure mourions mouriez meurent	mourrai	mourais	mourus	il est mort

mouvoir	mouvant	je meus tu meus il meut ns. mouvons vs. mouvez ils meuvent	meuve meuves meuve mouvions mouviez meuvent	mouvrai	mouvais	mus	j'ai mu
119							
naître	naissant	je nais tu nais il naît ns. naissons vs. naissez ils naissent	naisse naisses naisse naissions naissiez naissent	naîtrai	naissais	naquis	je suis né

nuire –
like luire

obtenir –
like tenir

offrir –
like ouvrir

63

INFINITIVE	PRES. PARTIC.	PRES. INDIC.	PRES. SUBJUN.	FUTURE	IMPERFECT	PASSÉ SIMPLE	PERFECT
ouvrir	ouvrant	j'ouvre tu ouvres il ouvre ns. ouvrons vs. ouvrez ils ouvrent	ouvre ouvres ouvre ouvrions ouvriez ouvrent	ouvrirai	ouvrais	ouvris	j'ai ouvert
120							
paraître — like connaître							
partir	partant	je pars tu pars il part ns. partons vs. partez ils partent	parte partes parte partions partiez partent	partirai	partais	partis	je suis parti
parvenir — like venir							
peindre — like craindre							

permettre —
like mettre

plaindre —
like craindre

plaire	plaisant	je plais tu plais il plaît ns. plaisons vs. plaisiez ils plaisent	plaise plaises plaise plaisions plaisiez plaisent	plairai	plaisais	plus	j'ai plu
pleuvoir	pleuvant	il pleut	il pleuve	il pleuvra	il pleuvait	il plut	il a plu
pouvoir	pouvant	je peux (puis) tu peux il peut ns. pouvons vs. pouvez ils peuvent	puisse puisses puisse puissions puissiez puissent	pourrai	pouvais	pus	j'ai pu
prendre	prenant	je prends tu prends	prenne prennes	prendrai	prenais	pris	j'ai pris

poursuivre —
like suivre

INFINITIVE	PRES. PARTIC.	PRES. INDIC.	PRES. SUBJUN.	FUTURE	IMPERFECT	PASSÉ SIMPLE	PERFECT
		il prend ns. prenons vs. prenez ils prennent	prenne prenions preniez prennent				
produire — like conduire							
promettre — like mettre							
121							
recevoir	recevant	je reçois tu reçois il reçoit ns. recevons vs. recevez ils reçoivent	reçoive reçoives reçoive recevions receviez reçoivent	recevrai	recevais	reçus	j'ai reçu
reconnaître — like connaître							
recueillir — like cueillir							

reprendre –
like prendre

résoudre	résolvant	je résous tu résous il résout ns. résolvons vs. résolvez ils résolvent	résolve résolves résolve résolvions résolviez résolvent	résoudrai	résolvais	résolus	j'ai résolu

revenir –
like venir

rire	riant	je ris tu ris il rit ns. rions vs. riez ils rient	rie ries rie riions riiez rient	rirai	rirais	ris	j'ai ri
rompre	rompant	je romps tu romps il rompt ns. rompons vs. rompez ils rompent	rompe rompes rompe rompions rompiez rompent	romprai	rompais	rompis	j'ai rompu

INFINITIVE	PRES. PARTIC.	PRES. INDIC.	PRES. SUBJUN.	FUTURE	IMPERFECT	PASSÉ SIMPLE	PERFECT
122							
savoir	sachant	je sais	sache	saurai	savais	sus	j'ai su
		tu sais	saches				
		il sait	sache				
		ns. savons	sachions				
		vs. savez	sachiez				
		ils savent	sachent				
sentir, servir – like dormir							
sortir – like partir							
souffrir – like ouvrir							
suffire	suffisant	je suffis	suffise	suffirai	suffisais	suffis	j'ai suffi
		tu suffis	suffises				
		il suffit	suffise				
		ns. suffisons	suffisions				
		vs. suffisez	suffisiez				
		ils suffisent	suffisent				

suivre	suivant	je suis tu suis il suit ns. suivons vs. suivez ils suivent	suive suives suive suivions suiviez suivent	suivrai	suivais	suivis	j'ai suivi
surprendre – like prendre							
survivre – like vivre							
123 se taire	se taisant	je me tais tu te tais il se tait ns. ns. taisons vs. vs. taisez ils se taisent	me taise te taises se taise ns. taisions vs. taisiez se taisent	me tairai	me taisais	me tus	je me suis tu
tenir	tenant	je tiens tu tiens il tient ns. tenons vs. tenez ils tiennent	tienne tiennes tienne tenions teniez tiennent	tiendrai	tenais	tins	j'ai tenu

124

INFINITIVE	PRES. PARTIC.	PRES. INDIC.	PRES. SUBJUN.	FUTURE	IMPERFECT	PASSÉ SIMPLE	PERFECT
vaincre	vainquant	je vaincs tu vaincs il vainc ns. vainquons vs. vainquez ils vainquent	vainque vainques vainque vainquions vainquiez vainquent	vaincrai	vainquais	vainquis	j'ai vaincu
valoir	valant	je vaux tu vaux il vaut ns. valons vs. valez ils valent	vaille vailles vaille vaillions vailliez vaillent	vaudrai	valais	valus	j'ai valu
venir	venant	je viens tu viens il vient ns. venons vs. venez ils viennent	vienne viennes vienne venions veniez viennent	viendrai	venais	vins	je suis venu

Infinitif	Participe présent	Présent	Subjonctif	Futur	Imparfait	Passé simple	Passé composé
vêtir	vêtant	je vêts tu vêts il vêt ns. vêtons vs. vêtez ils vêtent	vête vêtes vête vêtions vêtiez vêtent	vêtirai	vêtais	vêtis	j'ai vêtu
vivre	vivant	je vis tu vis il vit ns. vivons vs. vivez ils vivent	vive vives vive vivions viviez vivent	vivrai	vivais	vécus	j'ai vécu
voir	voyant	je vois tu vois il voit ns. voyons vs. voyez ils voient	voie voies voie voyions voyiez voient	verrai	voyais	vis	j'ai vu
vouloir	voulant	je veux tu veux il veut ns. voulons vs. voulez ils veulent	veuille veuilles veuille voulions vouliez veuillent	voudrai	voulais	voulus	j'ai voulu

125 Agreement of subject and verb

The subject agrees with the verb in number and person

Collective nouns have the verb in the singular if the sense of the noun is general and indeterminate.

La cohue menaça l'orateur	The mob threatened the speaker

Otherwise if the plurality is stressed the verb will be plural

Une assemblée de bêtes diverses suivaient le musicien	A crowd of different animals followed the musician

Similarly — **la plupart, un grand nombre, une quantité de . . .** will generally have a plural verb

La plupart des enfants étaient partis	The majority of the children had left

126 Subjects linked by **ou** or **ni**. If the linking emphasises the plural idea, the verb should be plural

Ni l'argent ni l'importance ne nous assurent le bonheur	Neither money nor importance guarantee happiness

Note: The verb is singular if a number of subjects are co-ordinated by **tout** or **rien** used collectively

La pluie, le vent, la brume, tout la faisait frissonner	Rain, wind, mist, anything made her shiver

127 Inversion of subject and verb

(a) This will obviously happen in most direct questions, as it does in English

Combien avez-vous payé?	How much did you pay?
Avez-vous déjà visité Nice?	Have you already been to Nice?

(b) With verbs of 'saying' after words of direct speech. Note that this is obligatory in French

'Nous serons prêts dans une heure', dit-il	'We shall be ready in an hour', he said

(c) Frequently in relative clauses introduced by **que** or **où**

Les arbres qu'avaient plantés mes aïeux	The trees my ancestors had planted

| Le lac où nageait autrefois mon oncle | The lake in which my uncle used to swim in former days |

(d) Sometimes in other clauses with **que**

| Quoi qu'en pensent mes voisins | Whatever my neighbours may think about it |
| Elle était plus émue que ne pensaient ses collègues | She was more moved than her colleagues thought |

(e) After **aussi** meaning 'therefore', after **à peine, peut-être**

Aussi a-t-il reçu une somme énorme	Therefore he received an enormous sum
A peine avait-il vu le vaisseau	Scarcely had he seen the vessel
Peut-être avait-il soupçonné qu'elle était sortie	Perhaps he had suspected that she had gone out

128 Faire

(a) = to have a thing done

| Il s'est fait bâtir une maison | He has had a house built for himself |
| Le gérant a fait monter les valises | The manager has had the bags brought up |

(b) If there is only one object of the verbal idea there is no difference from the English construction

| Je l'ai fait venir | I made him come |

(c) If however there are two objects, i.e. both **faire** and the following infinitive have an object, the object of **faire** is preceded by **à** (or the appropriate pronoun is used)

Thus:

On le fit entrer	They made him come in
On lui fit ouvrir la porte	They made him open the door
Elle fit écrire l'exercice à l'élève	She made the pupil write the exercise

(d) Note the omission of the reflexive pronoun after **faire**

| Il les fit asseoir | He made them sit down |

129 'It is', 'it was' etc.

Use **il est** etc.

(a) to tell time of day

| Il est dix heures | It is 10 o'clock |
| Il est midi et quart | It is quarter past twelve |

(b) with **il est temps**

| **Il est temps de partir** | It is time to leave |

(c) referring forward to a following idea

| **Il est impossible de l'apprendre par cœur** | It is impossible to learn it by heart |
| **Il était évident que le patron le savait déjà** | It was clear that the boss already knew |

Use **c'est** etc. in all other cases

It refers back

| **Ces femmes ne seront jamais satisfaites – ce n'est pas possible** | These women will never be satisfied – it is not possible |

It is used when the complement is not an adjective

| **Un miaulement terrible s'ensuivit; c'était un chat, tombé dans un piège** | A terrible caterwauling ensued – it was a cat caught in a trap |

130 Impersonal verbs

(a) the weather

Il fait beau (temps)	It is fine (weather)
Il fait mauvais (temps)	It is bad weather
Il fait chaud, froid	It is hot, cold
Il fait jour, nuit	It is light, dark
Il fait du vent	It is windy
Il fait du brouillard	It is foggy
pleuvoir	to rain
geler	to freeze
grêler	to hail
venter	to blow

Note: **geler** can be used personally in the sense of to be very cold

| **je gèle** | I am very cold |

(b) **il y a**   there is   **il y avait**   there was

il est   **il était** (the usual introduction to fairy tale: **Il était une fois**)

(c) **falloir**   **il faut** etc.

(d) il s'agit de . . .	it is a question (matter) of . . . etc.
(e) il vaut mieux	it is better
(f) il s'est passé/il est arrivé	there has happened

(g) 'It is' + adjective + infinitive

| Il est impossible de savoir si c'est vrai | It is impossible to know whether it is true |

131 Infinitive

1. Without a preposition

(a) modal verbs (see paragraph 150)

| Nous ne pouvions pas venir | We were unable to come |

(b) after **aller, partir, venir, savoir, croire**

Il est parti chercher le médecin	He has left to get the doctor
Elle est venue aider ma mère	She has come to help my mother
Il croit être sûr	He thinks he is sure
Je sais jouer du piano	I can (know how to) play the piano

but:

| venir de faire | to have just done |
| Je viens d'acheter un imperméable | I have just bought a raincoat |

2. Without a preposition or with à after **aimer** and **penser**

| J'aime à boire une bière le soir | I like to have a beer in the evening |
| J'aime me promener tout seul | I like to go for a walk by myself |

Penser à (faire) has the sense of 'not to forget to'

| Pense à fermer la porte | Remember to shut the door |

3. Introduced by à after the following verbs
apprendre, commencer, se décider, encourager, enseigner, s'intéresser, se mettre, se résoudre, réussir, songer

Il recommença à chanter	He began to sing again
Nous nous sommes décidés à l'accompagner	We made up our minds to go with him
Elle réussit à l'apprendre	She succeeded in learning it

4. Introduced by **de** after the following verbs
**s'aviser, décider, commander, conseiller, demander, défendre
(forbid), dire, s'efforcer, s'empresser, essayer, exiger, interdire,
permettre, persuader, prier, promettre, rêver, tâcher, se souvenir**

Il décida de le lire à haute voix	He decided to read it aloud
On le pria de rester là	He was asked to stay there

5. **C'est à toi de parler** — It's your turn to speak
   A vous de jouer! — Your turn to play

132 English verbal forms in '-ing' and how to cope with some of them.
Perhaps the most difficult idea that the English beginner in French has
to master is that French has no tenses which use a present participle to
indicate continuous action

Il va	He is going
Ils entrent	They are entering
Nous nagions	We were swimming

One way of stressing continuity in French is by using **en train de**
Il était en train de sonner la retraite	He was sounding the retreat

Note: It is true that the French may use a present participle after **aller**
but the foreigner is advised to know of, but not imitate this
Un fiacre allait trottinant	A cab was clip-clopping along

133 The present participle may be used as an adjective as in English
Des vagues étincelantes	Sparkling waves

134 Beware 'after' + verbal form in '-ing'. In French **après** requires a
perfect infinitive
Après avoir lavé la cour, elle ferma la porte	After washing the yard, she closed the door

135 *Note:* ways of rendering 'by' + verbal form in '-ing'
L'appétit vient en mangeant	Appetite comes by eating
A force de chercher son sac elle a fini par le trouver	By looking hard for her bag she finally found it
Nous avons commencé par chanter la Marseillaise	We began by singing the Marseillaise

136 'When' + verbal form in '-ing'

En courant		When running along the
Alors qu'elle courait	dans la rue	road, she stumbled
Lorsqu'elle courait	elle trébucha	

137 English uses the verbal form in '-ing' with conjunctions and sometimes alone, where French has a full clause

Bien qu'il ne manquât pas de courage, il dut se retirer	Although not lacking in courage, he had to withdraw

138 Sometimes the English use of the verbal form in '-ing' may not be quite logical — 'Drawing his sword he cut down the curtain' will be rendered more logically by

Quand il eut tiré son épée	
Après avoir tiré son épée	il trancha le rideau
Il tira son épée et trancha le rideau	

139 *Note:*

Il réussit à trouver la bague	He succeeded in finding the ring
Ils se mirent à courir	They began running
J'ai pensé à le conseiller	I thought of advising him
Il ne s'agit pas de payer	It's not a question of paying
Défense de fumer	Smoking forbidden
Je n'aime pas danser	I don't like dancing
Rire est une chose, ricaner en est une autre	Laughing is one thing, sneering is another
Je ne veux pas qu'il aille à mon appartement	I don't want him going to my flat
Assise à la fenêtre, elle observait les passants	Sitting at the window, she observed the passers-by

140 After some verbs expressing seeing and hearing the verbal idea in '-ing' is rendered by an infinitive without à or **de**

Je l'ai entendu ronfler	I heard him snoring
Elle le vit venir vers elle	She saw him coming towards her
J'entends venir quelqu'un	I can hear someone coming

Notes on tenses with particular reference to different usage in French and English

141 Present

1. There is no continuous present in French

Il va He is going

2. With clauses using **depuis** and **il y a** (ago) French uses the present for an action which is continuing in the present even though it began in the past

Il y a dix ans que j'apprends l'anglais

J'apprends l'anglais depuis dix ans

} I have been learning English for ten years (and I still am)

This does not apply when the verb is negative

Il y a dix ans que je ne l'ai pas vu

Je ne l'ai pas vu depuis dix ans

} I haven't seen him for ten years

142 Future

If the main clause verb is in the future or the imperative the verb in a subordinate clause of **time** will be in the future

Nous partirons quand il viendra We shall start when he comes

Entrez aussitôt que vous serez prêt Come in as soon as you are ready

On le laissera entrer après qu'il aura payé They'll let him in after he has paid

143 Perfect

Is regularly used in colloquial French to express a single completed action in the past. Literary French will use the *passé simple*

Est-ce que tu l'as vu venir? Did you see him coming?

144 Passé simple

Used to advance the story a step in the past, to indicate the next happening in a narrative (hence its other name – the *passé historique*). This tense has ceased to be used in spoken French. For examples see the verbs in italics in the passage below (section **146**)

145 Imperfect

1. With clauses using **depuis** and **il y avait** French uses the imperfect
   for action which had begun in the past and was continuing at the
   time of speaking (cf. use of present above)

   Il y avait longtemps qu'il
   pratiquait cet art
   Il pratiquait cet art depuis
   longtemps
   } He had been practising that art
   for a long time (and was still
   doing so)

2. describes the background to actions in the past

3. describes continuous action in the past (hence its other name
   passé continu)

4. describes habitual action in the past; hence it is often used where
   English would have 'used to'

   Il allait souvent au théâtre   He often used to go to the
   theatre

5. Can be used to express a wish

   Ah! s'il transmettait son génie à   Ah! If he were to hand on his
   son fils!   genius to his son!

146 Some examples of the use of the *passé simple* and the imperfect can be seen in

Nous traversions la forêt depuis deux heures. Il pleuvait toujours à
verse: les gouttes de pluie tombaient dru et rendaient de plus en plus
lourds nos ponchos. Même les ânes qui allaient généralement au trot
lorsqu'ils s'approchaient du village, traînaient le pas. Soudain un coup
de fusil *retentit* et le guide nous *fit* signe de nous arrêter. Il *resta* là
immobile, essayant de distinguer quelque chose parmi le bruit de la
pluie. Nous ne pouvions rien voir au delà de la faible lueur que
jetaient nos lanternes. Enfin le guide *décida* qu'il n'y avait plus de
danger et nous *fit* continuer notre voyage.

147 Passé antérieur

1. In clauses introduced by **quand, lorsque, dès que, aussitôt que,**
   après que the *passé antérieur* is used where English would have the
   pluperfect, provided that the main clause verb is in the *passé simple*

   Lorsqu'il eut vu ce drame, il   When he had seen this play he
   résolut d'en écrire un meilleur   decided to write a better one

2. The *passé antérieur* is also used to express the speed of an action

| En un clin d'oeil il eut tout remis en place | In a twinkling of an eye he had got everything back in place. |

148 Passé surcomposé

This is a tense used mainly in spoken French. It is the perfect of avoir + another past participle and has no equivalent in English, where it is best rendered by the pluperfect

| Il est parti quand il a eu fini son travail | He left when he had finished his job. |

149 Students sometimes confuse tenses with **quand** and **si**

Tenses with **si** are therefore given

Si vous l'aidez un peu il ira plus vite	If you help him a bit he will get on more quickly
Si vous l'aidiez un peu il irait plus vite	If you were to help him a bit he would get on more quickly
Si vous l'aviez aidé un peu il serait allé plus vite	If you had helped him a bit he would have got on more quickly

Note: **si** = what if, supposing that

| Si on allait au théâtre? | What if we were to go to the theatre? |

150 Modal verbs

When with another verb, as they usually are, these verbs require no preposition with the following infinitive

| Je veux y aller | I want to go |

Devoir   1. 'must'

Je dois y aller ce soir	I must go tonight
Nous devrons y aller demain	We shall have to go tomorrow
J'ai dû y aller	I have had to go
Elle a dû l'oublier	She must have forgotten it

2. 'ought' (in conditional tenses)

| Nous devrions payer la note | We ought to pay the bill |
| Nous aurions dû payer la note | We ought to have paid the bill |

3. 'am to', 'was to' (in present and imperfect)

Je dois y aller demain	I am to go there tomorrow
Il devait régler l'affaire	He was bound to settle the matter

Pouvoir   1. 'can' (physical ability)

Il ne peut pas nager parce qu'il a une crampe	He can't swim because he's got cramp

Note: **savoir** - 'can' in the sense of 'having learnt how to'

Il sait nager	He can swim

2. 'may' (possibility or permission)

Tu peux sortir quand tu auras fini tes devoirs	You may go out when you've done your homework

Vouloir   'to want', 'wish', 'like'

Je veux qu'il s'en aille	I want him to go away

Note use in *conditional* when English might have *present*: e.g. in shopping

Je voudrais un demi-kilo de sucre	I want half a kilo of sugar

And with **bien** to emphasise the wish

Je voudrais bien y aller	I **would** like to go
Veuillez bien me dire	Be so good as to tell me

Falloir   'must', 'have to' (impersonal)

Il faut que nous allions au marché	We must go to the market

151 Passive voice

Is formed in French as it is in English — the verb 'to be' + past participle

Examples

Present	**Je suis agacé**	I am upset
Future	**Tu seras puni**	You will be punished
Perfect	**Il a été trahi**	He has been betrayed
Imperfect	**Nous étions accompagnés**	We were accompanied
Passé simple	**Ils furent attaqués**	They were attacked
Conditional	**Vous seriez mordu(es)**	You would be bitten
Pluperfect	**Ils avaient été battus**	They had been beaten

There is one different and difficult point of usage. Consider the following

	Subject		*Direct object*	
Verb in *active* voice	A cat	scratched	me	
Verb in *passive* voice	I	was scratched		by a cat

This can be rendered in French

| *Active* | **Un chat m'a égratigné** |
| *Passive* | **J'ai été égratigné par un chat** |

The direct object in the sentence with the verb in the Active voice becomes the subject in the sentence with the verb in the Passive voice. So far the usage is parallel in the two languages. But English does not always follow this pattern.

| *Active* | His father gave him a car |
| *Passive* | He was given a car by his father |

In this 'Active' sentence the direct object is 'a car', and 'him' (= to him) is the indirect object. Yet in the 'Passive' sentence the *indirect* object has been made into the subject.

Here is another example:

> I told him the story
> He was told the story by me

This practice is not possible in French. The *indirect* object of a verb in the Active voice cannot become the subject of the verb in the Passive voice. This calls for special care with verbs like **dire, permettre, promettre, ordonner, défendre** (= forbid), **offrir** because the personal object in the Active voice with these verbs is an *indirect* one. e.g.

J'ai dit à ma mère que . . .	I told my mother that . . .
Nous lui permettons de sortir	We allow him to go out
Vous avez offert à votre fils	You offered your son a
un choix raisonnable	reasonable choice

Consequently, the Passive idea in English will have to be rendered *either* by turning the idea into the Active voice, thus

I was forbidden to go   **On m'a défendu d'y aller**

or in some cases by using an *impersonal* construction

                Il m'a été défendu d'aller

152 *Note:* other French constructions where English might use the Passive

On dit que . . .	It is said that
Ça se comprend	That is understood
Terrain à vendre	Plot for sale (to be sold)
Cette expression ne se traduit pas facilement	That expression cannot be translated easily

Uses of the Subjunctive

As a general guide: the use of the subjunctive implies that what is happening or being described is considered from the point of view of some emotion like desire, fear, gladness, uncertainty — but this is only a general guide.

153 **used alone**

In modern French it is introduced by **que** except in fixed expressions like — **Ainsi soit-il! Vive le roi!**

It can express: *an order* in the 3rd person singular

Qu'il le fasse vite	Let him do it quickly

a wish

Qu'on le cherche tout de suite	Have him sent for at once

a concession

Je ne l'ai pas rédigé de cette façon, que je sache	I did not draw it up like that, so far as I am aware

154 **after certain conjunctions**

quoique **bien que**	although
à moins que . . . . ne	unless
de crainte que . . . . ne **de peur que . . . . ne**	for fear that
avant que	before
pour que **afin que**	in order that
pourvu que	provided that

de façon que ⎫ de sorte que ⎬ jusqu'à ce que	in such a way that until
Quoiqu'elle ne l'aimât plus elle resta avec lui	Although she did not love him any more she stayed with him

155 after **qui que** (whoever), **quoi que** (whatever)

Qui que tu sois, voici ton maître; il l'est, le fut ou le doit être	Whoever you are, here is your master; he is, was, or will be. (Inscription on a statue of Cupid)

156 in 'however' clauses — si + adjective + **que**

Si beau qu'il soit . . .	However handsome he may be . .

157 after the following impersonal verbs

**il est possible (impossible) que . . . il faut que . . . il vaut mieux que . . .
il semble que . . . il est temps que . . .**

Il vaut mieux qu'il parte tout de suite	He'd better start out at once
Il est temps que tu partes	It's time for you to go

But **il est probable que . . .** and **il semble que . . .** with a personal pronoun + indicative

Il semble qu'il ait raison
Il me semble qu'il a raison
Nevertheless **il paraît que** + indicative

158 after main clause verbs expressing surprise, indignation, admiration, wish, doubt, fear, command, permission, forbidding

Je regrette qu'il en soit ainsi	I'm sorry things are like this
Il défendra qu'on aille les voir	He won't allow them to have visitors
Dis-lui qu'il parte bientôt	Tell him to start out soon
Je crains qu'il ne* soit mort	I fear he may be dead
Nous voulons que vous ayez un véritable succès	We want you to have a real success
Il est douteux que nous le fassions	It is doubtful whether we shall do it

Note: the **ne** after verbs of fearing but only when the 'fear' verb is in a positive statement

Elle ne craignait pas qu'on la bousculât	She wasn't afraid of being jostled

159 **espérer** is followed by the indicative

J'espère que vous viendrez	I hope you will come

160 after verbs of saying or thinking used negatively or in question form, because they suggest a doubt

Je ne crois pas qu'il fasse de telles choses	I don't think he does things like that
Pensez-vous qu'elle ait fait cela?	Do you think she has done that?

But if the subject of both clauses is the same person, use the infinitive

Croyez-vous pouvoir le faire?	Do you think you can do it?

161 in adjectival clauses

(a) after a superlative

C'est le plus grand homme que j'aie connu	He is the greatest man I have known

(b) after **premier, dernier, seul, unique**

Voici la seule femme qui sache le faire	Here is the only woman who can do it

(c) depending on a negative

Il n'y a rien qui soit si simple	There's nothing which is so simple
Je ne vois personne qui puisse l'aider	I don't see anyone who can help him

(d) when there is a sense of purpose in the adjectival clause

1. **On va chercher un guide qui contienne ces renseignements**	We are going to look for a guide which has this information
but 2. **Voici un guide qui contient . . .**	Here is a guide which contains . .

In (1) there is no certainty that such a guide exists but if it does, it is our purpose to find it.

In (2) we know the book exists. We are merely describing what it contains.

162 Tenses in the subjunctive: modern French even in literary style makes little use of the imperfect and pluperfect subjunctive, except in the 3rd person singular. When a past tense of the subjunctive seems to be needed because the main clause verb is in the past, the present subjunctive is generally used; sometimes the perfect if the sense indicates it.

Ils voulaient que le notaire $\left\{ \begin{array}{l} \text{1. lût} \\ \text{2. lise} \end{array} \right\}$ le testament

They wanted the lawyer to read the will

1. is a written form, 2. the more usual spoken one.

---

163 Position of pronouns with a verb

(a) ordinary pronouns stand before the verb they refer to unless the verb is a positive imperative (i.e. telling someone to do something)

Vous le lui prêterez
Vous allez le lui prêter $\Big\}$ You will lend him (her) it

Ne leur en donnez pas   Don't give them any

Je voudrais vous les présenter   I should like to introduce them to you

Elles nous connaissent déjà   They already know us

With a *positive* imperative this is not so; the pronoun then follows the verb and is hyphenated to it

Donnez-les à ma soeur   Give them to my sister

Parlez-lui tout de suite   Speak to him (her) at once

Also, **me** or **te** is not used as the object of a positive imperative; instead, **moi** or **toi** is used if, as is usual, it is the concluding idea in the command.

Donnez-moi du café   Give me some coffee

Donnez-le-moi   Give it to me

Rappelle-toi ce que je t'ai dit   Remember what I told you

Perhaps the reason for this is the reluctance of the French to end an emphatic idea like an imperative with a weak sounding **me** or **te** when the stronger **moi** or **toi** is available. When, however, there is another idea at the end of the imperative **moi** or **toi** is, obviously, unnecessary. Consequently

Donnez-m'en   Give me some

(b) if there is more than one pronoun *before* a verb the order can be determined by the following rough and ready mnemonic

	Explanation
1 before 2	1st person before 2nd person pronouns
2 before 3	2nd person before 3rd person pronouns
(A before D)	If both pronouns are 3rd person, Accusative (direct object) before Dative (indirect object) pronoun
y before en	

Thus:

Je m'en doutais bien	I suspected as much
Il nous l'a dit	He told us so
Il vous l'a dit **Il te l'a dit**	He told you so
Il le lui a dit	He told him (her) so
Il lui en a parlé	He spoke to him (her) about it
Il leur en a parlé	He spoke to them about it
Il y en a	There are some

164 **que** is used to avoid the repetition of a conjunction

    Quand nous sommes arrivés et   When we arrived and saw her
    que nous l'avons vue

165 Use of **capital letters** in English but not with the French equivalent
    (a) **je** has a small letter (unless it is the first word in the sentence)

    (b) adjectives of nationality and the names of languages have small letters

        C'est un navire français   It is a French ship
        Elle apprend le grec   She is learning Greek

But when the nationality adjective is used as a noun to indicate the people of the country it has a capital letter
    Les Français ont une république   The French have a republic

    (c) common geographical nouns, part of a geographical name, have a small letter
    l'océan Atlantique   The Atlantic Ocean

(d) nouns showing rank or profession if followed by a proper noun have a small letter.

le docteur Legros	Dr. Legros
le général Dubois	General Dubois

(e) words such as **rue, boulevard, place** in names have a small letter

Il demeure place Saint-Antoine

le boulevard Saint-Michel

Index

References are to paragraph numbers

91